Three Blue Beans

ANOTHER YEAR IN HAIKU

Hamish Ironside

With linocuts by
MUNGO M^cCOSH

IRON
PRESS

Published in 2018 by IRON Press,
5 Marden Terrace, Cullercoats, North Shields,
Northumberland, NE30 4PD, UK
Telephone: +44 (0)191 253 1901
Email: ironpress@blueyonder.co.uk
www.ironpress.co.uk

ISBN 978-0-9954579-3-5

Printed in the UK by Short Run Press, Exeter,
on 80 gsm Munken Premium paper

Typeset in Walbaum and Gill Sans

IRON Press books are distributed by NBN International
and represented by Inpress Limited,
Churchill House, 12 Mosley Street,
Newcastle upon Tyne, NE1 1DE
Telephone: +44 (0)191 2308104
www.inpressbooks.co.uk

for my mother and father

Contents

Acknowledgements

Thanks to Matthew Hollis, Fabian Ironside and Matthew Paul for helping to sort the wheat from the chaff. Thanks to Pete Mortimer and Kate Jones at IRON Press for unflagging support and good cheer. Thanks to Mungo McCosh for artistry with integrity. Thanks to Julia and Aspen for all the rest of it.

Inching
from dark to dark—
seaslug.

KATO GYODAI
(*tr. Lucien Stryk and Takashi Ikemoto*)

JANUARY

on a grey wall
the grey graffito:
slut

my daughter scolds me
for singing about the time
I shot that old man down

a street penny
pregnant
with a pennyweight of rain

once the favour
is over, the resentment
can begin

the new clapping game—
she tells me no one knows
where it came from

a child stares at me
consulting the *OED*
like I'm up to no good

crescent moon—
all those things
she might not tell me

in fading light
the allure of a path
that takes us off the map

from another room
my wife asks me
which century we're in

in a bookshop
I make myself find
the typo I missed

cold sun—
the nuclear power station
emits a puff of starlings

FEBRUARY

in a classroom
the daughters of wealth
rehearse 'Smells Like Teen Spirit'

crossing the cemetery
light sent by stars
before the dead were born

shorten the stalks
so they can live longer
a dying friend said

running up a muddy hill
still nursing
an ancient grievance

hilltop puddle—
starlings flicker
like super 8

yearning for sleep—
and when it comes
I dream of sleeping

a skylark queries:
'in what way, exactly,
am I "daffy"?'

my mind slackens off
to let my fingers
remember a chord

MARCH

a pubic hair
pirouetting
into the plughole

the ironing board
the exercise mat
the contested space

working weekend—
the *Oxford Spelling Dictionary*
shouts *asshole* at me

a piece of work
I could do in my sleep
keeps me awake

spring dawn—
a plume of steam
writhes into sunlight

the washed-up carcass
seems more plesiosaurus
than whale or porpoise

a gannet sleeps
just beyond the reach
of a ruined sea

APRIL

St Ives to Zennor
seems longer driving
than it was running

the waitress rhapsodizes
about living by the coast;
a dog shits on the decking

Good Friday—
a man mimes a cricket stroke
with an umbrella

burst blister—
erogenous redness
of the underskin

spring morning—
a yin and yang
of baby squirrels

brooding on money;
I shorten the swingball rope
to fit the garden

mouths of fish
gulping at the surface
as if drowning

around midnight
the moon shows up
looking lost and gaunt

the walk home from school—
I try to recall
how life began

in the library
a tramp studies a chess book,
his face an endgame

MAY

on my idle arm
a pair of flies
meet, mate and split

walking around the block
I spot my wife
coveting a Renault

a brown and white foal
safe in the lee
of the A317

intending 'future'
I see my hand
has written 'failure'

our nervous cat
seems so relaxed
in the neighbour's garden

a dream of Nick Drake—
the feeling when I wake
that he rides on

an old diary
starring people I barely remember
including myself

for good measure
the cash machine delivers
an electric shock

JUNE

teenagers oscillate
between the study room
and the children's room

past caring
the Saturday cyclist
in Marmite lycra

schoolgirl laughter—
I still think
it must be at me

June's long day—
light sticks to the edges
of antlers

a spider snares a wasp
with the overelaboration
of a Bond villain

in her newsreading voice
she tells me someone's selling my book
for a penny

elusive thoughts
quicksilver through my mind
pursued by words

'do not judge the worm'
(I tell my wife) 'who injects
his own head with sperm'

dentist's garden—
among pebbles and wild flowers,
a discarded bra

a virus shows me
the cracks in reality,
the vast world beyond

a hemisphere away
he calls me back
to say goodbye

JULY

the splendour of dust
in a shaft of sun—
she will not have it

my daughter asks
how I shall entertain myself
the day before Armageddon

pre-school children
flee the low-grade fun
of grandparents

bird of spring and autumn,
strange to see you fly
in all this heat

in the sea of grass
a golf ball husk
is a snail's coracle

the myth of pleasure . . .
Saturday night vomit
in Sunday morning rain

zombily driving
beside the river
the longest way home

tenth birthday—
the wind blows out the candles
before she can

brother and brother
each now a figment
of the other

that vaunted organ
the heart, at the wheel again
bumper to bumper

a small coin
of cloud—the moon
in the afternoon

mental health ward—
my wife asks how they'll know
I'm not a patient

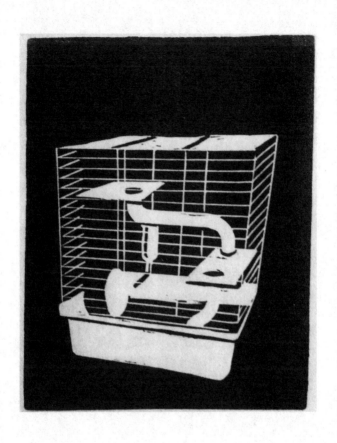

AUGUST

the empty box
of a pregnancy test
outside the girls' school

drive-thru safari—
a clot of cars accrues
for that prick-tease the tiger

magpies in a trap—
and us in our own cage
of craven politeness

went in a room
for an item of clothing
and left with a book

my joke is taken
through to the bedroom
for its autopsy

the river and I
both running
on empty

carpenter's pencil—
I sharpen it
with a chisel

in a wooden panel
of the courtroom of honour
it says *fuck around get killed*

sunny clouds—
khaki outfield
of an old season

at the charity shop
a cage with everything
but the chinchilla

autumn—
the smell of radiators
waking from a long sleep

Sunday night—
along wet pavement
a sprawl of green light

SEPTEMBER

the tent's blue wall
at dawn—a constellation
of dewdrops

climbing off the female,
the male pelican
can't suppress a yawn

new school year—
I hang back to watch my daughter
walking home alone

she calls an almond
a pecan—the new girl
at the bakery

riverside run
both of us struggling
to keep up with the other

from the New World
my brother speaks Fahrenheit
to my Celsius

cleaning my pen—
the ink of my youth
won't stop bleeding

autumn evening
made out of spring—
stratocumulus undulatus

all things must pass,
including my copy of
All Things Must Pass

we don't fix the light
but we do buy it
a new lampshade

OCTOBER

a mouldy Volkswagen
propped up on bricks
down a cul-de-sac

give a tramp a coin
to buy yourself some luck—
it doesn't work like that

autumn—
an old woman
twirling her pigtails

on the jumbotron
a slow-motion replay
of a man shouting 'fuck'

running in rain
letting my mind roam
across evolution

alone in the flat
I don't even know
my wife's star sign

in darkness
a lone aspen
calls to me

where the council estate
meets the meadow,
a beach mural

NOVEMBER

a needle
pulled through cloth—
the grebe's dive

after the cathedral
after the woods
explaining what rape is

starlings coalesce
on a church spire—
the dream of Eden

the Sainsbury's sign
lights up
the dirt within it

the men at the pool
don't know what to do
about Isis

breakfasting alone
I catch myself
planning a haiku

massed cloud at dusk
slumped beyond the town
my mountain to climb

fish tank—
the emptiness of life
without predation

children's playground
flanked by gravestones
waiting like parents

earthquakes in China
crammed into the corner
of the chip shop

DECEMBER

I crack the same joke
at the same time
as my mother-in-law

'the foetal life'—
the good old foetal life,
the life of Riley

cheap unbranded toys—
the businesswoman princess
and her anguished horse

anti-war march—
we join it for a few steps
to get to the shops

across the river
a heron takes off
like a tent blowing over

post office queue—
a guitar solo squeals
almost inaudibly

on her Boggle list,
KIND and LOVE; on mine,
LUST and ANAL

a dripping tap—
my mother's heart
and my own

added in red ink
on a missing cat poster:
'still lost'

a jaundiced moon
gets up close
and personal

sunlit rain—
my daughter figures
how long I've got left

the sound of my wife
doing jobs for her mother
that I do at home

the last light lost,
the green gone grey—
what am I waiting for?

About the author

Hamish Ironside was born in Reading in 1971. He now lives with his wife and daughter in Twickenham, which Wikipedia describes as 'a leafy affluent suburban area of south west London'. He takes no part in its affluence, but is well acquainted with its leafiness.

He works as a freelance editor and typesetter for publishers such as Faber & Faber, Bloomsbury and Routledge. In 2015, with Michael Fell, he founded Boatwhistle, a publisher of 'singular books for singular readers'.

Hamish's first book of haiku, *Our Sweet Little Time*, was published by IRON Press in 2009, and it is being reissued in 2018 to celebrate the publication of *Three Blue Beans*. Hamish won first prize in the British Haiku Awards for 2014. His longer poems have been published in *The Guardian*, *Poetry Review* and *Parnassus*, among others.

All of the haiku in *Three Blue Beans* are previously unpublished.

About the artist

Mungo McCosh was born in 1970. He studied fine art at St Martin's School of Art in London and in Glasgow before moving to Istanbul, where he lived for six years. The Crimean memorial church in that city has a rood screen painted by him. He now lives with his wife, the painter Phoebe Cope, and their two children in a remote house in the Scottish Borders surrounded by sheep and heather. He commutes 20 yards daily to his studio where he works as a painter, printmaker and architect manqué.

He has illustrated for publications as different as *Granta* and *Country Life*, and worked with a wide variety of publishers including Jonathan Cape, who in 2005 published *An Alphabet of Aunts*, an enjoyable collaboration with the literary agent Caroline Dawnay. In 2004 he worked as an embedded artist with the Argyll and Sutherland Highlanders in Iraq, and in 2007 and 2008 accompanied HRH the Prince of Wales as artist on official tours to Uganda, Turkey and the Caribbean. He likes ginger-coloured cats, Seljuk mosques, rice puddings and planting trees.

About the linocuts

The twelve pictures in this book are printed lithographically from linocuts commissioned from Mungo McCosh by the publisher.

The making of a linocut print typically takes several days. The process begins with Mungo drawing a design in pencil, which is transferred via tracing paper to the face of a piece of linoleum. Mungo then cuts away material from the plate using miniature gouges and chisels. Impressions are taken by rolling ink onto the surface of the lino and printing onto a sheet of paper using an antique cast-iron press. Several impressions of the developing print may be taken before Mungo is satisfied that the cutting of a print is finished.

Techniques used in linocut printmaking are closely related to those used to make woodcut prints, a form of relief printmaking that reached its apogee in Japan, making it a particularly appropriate medium to illustrate a collection of haiku.

Impressions of all of the illustrations in this book have been printed by Mungo on acid-free Japanese paper, signed and editioned by him. These (and many other prints) can be viewed or purchased at the artist's website, www.mungomccosh.com.

About the publisher

IRON Press is among the country's longest-established independent literary publishers. The press began in 1973 with *IRON Magazine*, which ran for 83 editions until 1997. Since 1975 we have brought out a regular list of individual collections of poetry, fiction and drama, plus anthologies ranging from *The Poetry of Perestroika* to *Limerick Nation*, *100 Island Poems* and *Cold Iron: Ghost Stories from the 21st Century*.

The press is one of the leading publishers of haiku in the UK. Since 2013 we have also run a regular IRON Press Festival round the harbour in our native Cullercoats. IRON in the Soul, our third festival, took place in Summer 2017.

We are delighted to be a member of Inpress Ltd, which was set up by Arts Council England to support independent literary publishers. Please visit our website (www.ironpress.co.uk) for full details of our titles and activities.